1·2·3 Draw People

People

A step-by-step guide by

Freddie Levin

You will need:

- a pencil
- an eraser (one of my most important art supplies!)
- a pencil sharpener
- lots of paper (recycle and re-use)
- colored pencils for finishing drawings
- a folder for saving your work
- a good light
- a comfortable place to draw

Now let's begin!

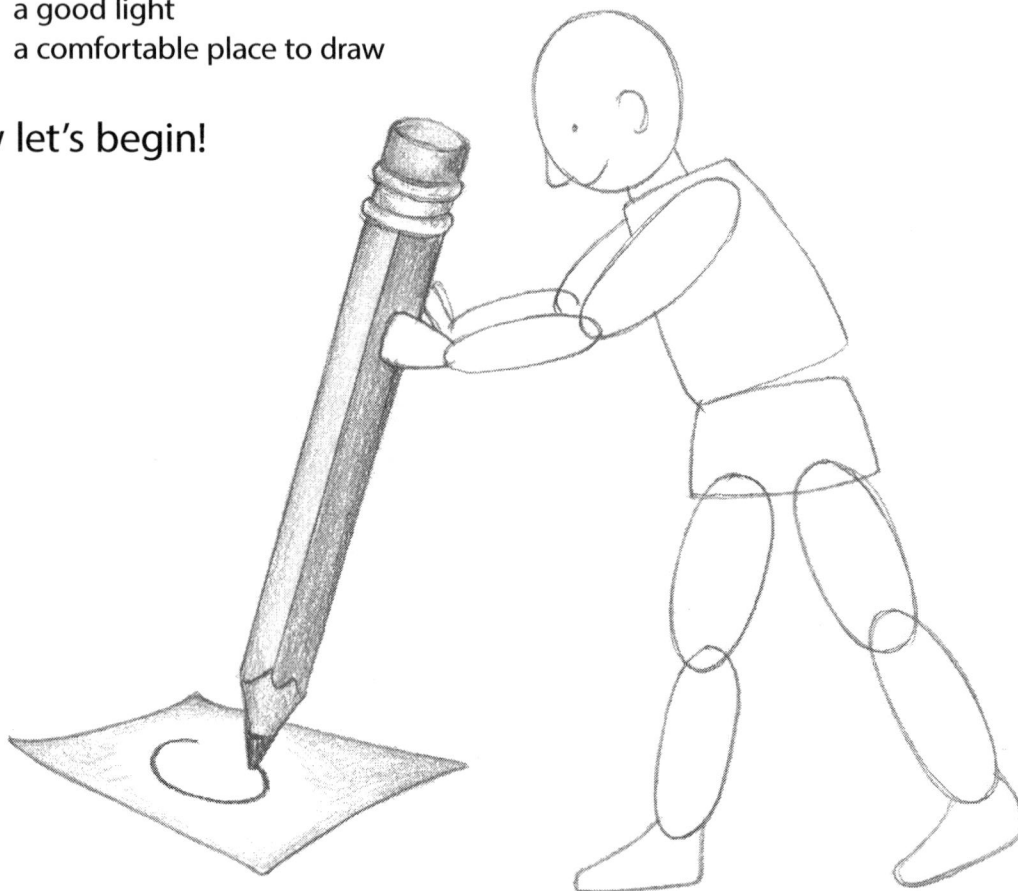

You can see the original color illustrations at 123draw.com/color

Library of Congress Cataloging-in-Publication Data (original edition)

Levin, Freddie.
  1-2-3 draw people / by Freddie Levin.
     p. cm.
  Includes index.
  ISBN _____ (pbk. : alk. paper)
  1. Human figure in art--Juvenile literature. 2. Colored pencil drawing-
-Technique--Juvenile literature. I. Title. II. Title: One-two-three draw
people. III. Title: Draw people.

NC765.L41 2007
704.9'42--dc22

              2006024867

Contents

Important Drawing Tips:

1   Draw lightly at first (SKETCH), so you can erase extra lines later.

2   The first few shapes are important. Notice the size, shape and positions of the first shapes.

3   To shade and color your drawing, start lightly and GRADUALLY make the color darker. Don't forget you can BLEND colors too.

4   Practice, practice, practice!

5   Have fun drawing people!

The Basics

The drawings in this book all begin with a few basic shapes. Learn these shapes and practice drawing them.

square

rectangle

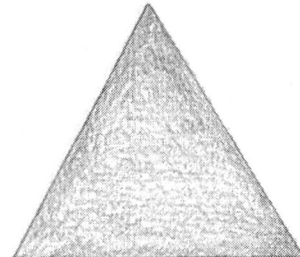
triangle

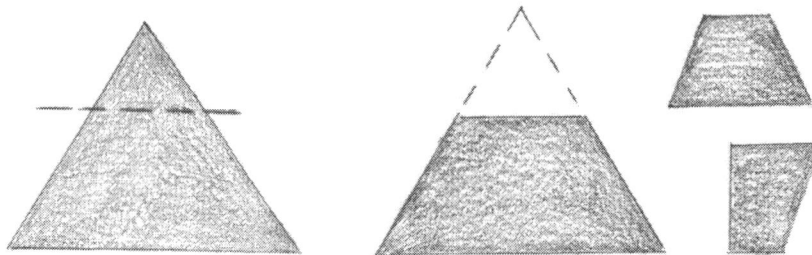

A trapezoid is a triangle with the top cut off.

A

B

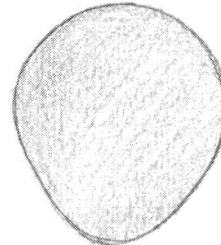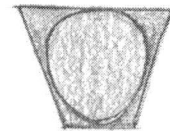
C

A   A circle fits in a square
B   An oval fits in a rectangle.
C   An egg shape fits in a trapezoid. We will be using lots of egg shapes for drawing heads.

Remember:

1   Draw lightly at first - SKETCH
2   Practice
3   Practice
4   Practice
5   Have fun drawing PEOPLE!

Drawing People

Let's look at some of the basic shapes and proportions for drawing people. We'll get into details later.

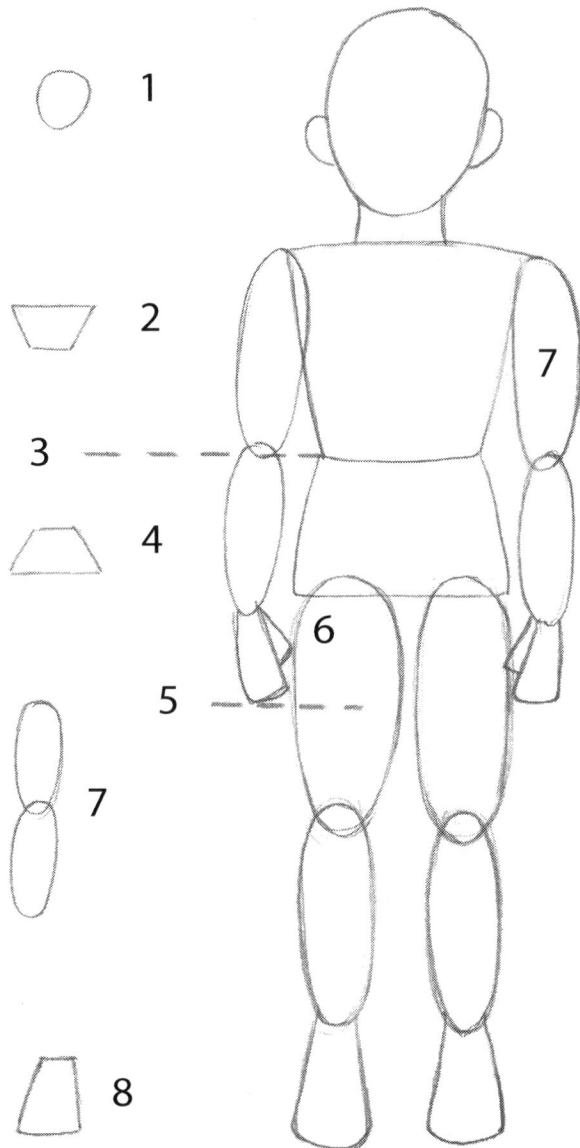

1 The head is egg-shaped.

2 The chest is a trapezoid.

3 Elbows are at the waist. Put your arms down at your sides. Notice where your elbows are.

4 From the waist to the beginning of the legs is the second trapezoid.

5 Put your hands down at your sides. Notice where your hands are. They are at the middle of your thigh.

6 Notice on which side of your hand your thumb is.

7 Arms and legs are ovals. They are connected at elbows and knees.

8 The basic shape of hands and feet is a trapezoid.

Basic Person
Front view

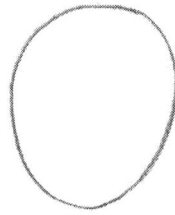

Before we draw people in action, we will draw some basic figures.

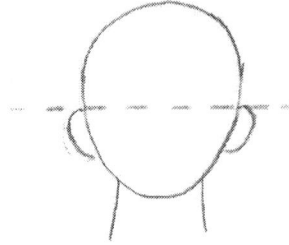

1   All the people in this book start the same way: Draw an egg.

2   Add ears. Draw two lines for the neck.

3   Draw a trapezoid for the chest.

4   Add a second trapezoid to complete the body.

5   Draw the upper arms and legs.

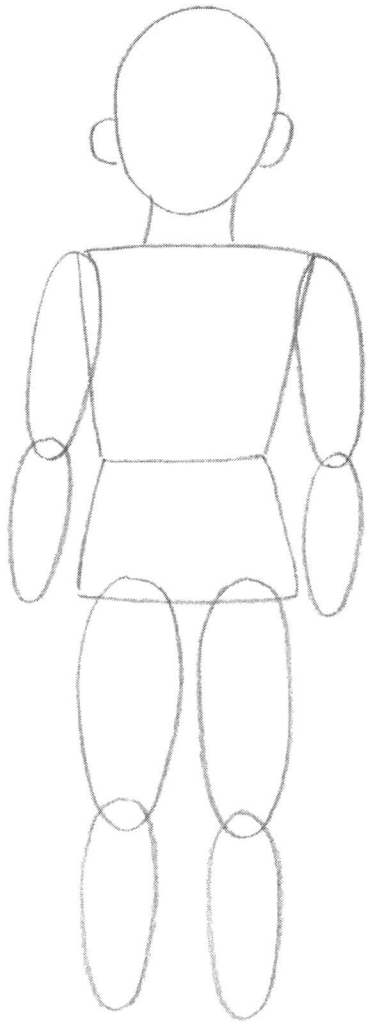

6 Draw the lower arms and legs.

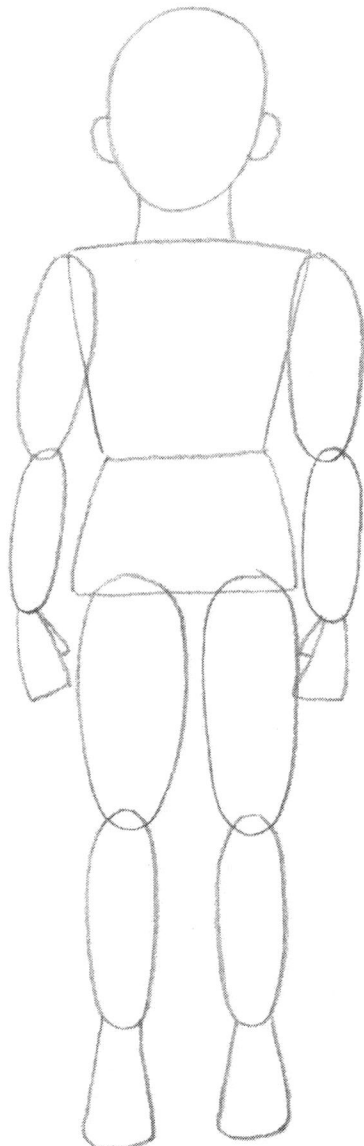

7 Add hands and feet.

Basic person
Side view

A side view of a head is called a profile.

1 Start with an egg. Notice the angle. It is different from the front view head.

2 Add two lines for a neck.

3 Draw the chest. Notice that it is a somewhat different trapezoid shape than the front view.

4 Add a second trapezoid to complete the body.

5 Draw the upper arms and legs. This person is walking so the arms and legs are swinging out away from the body.

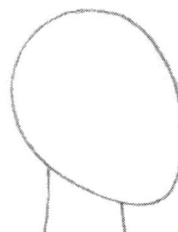

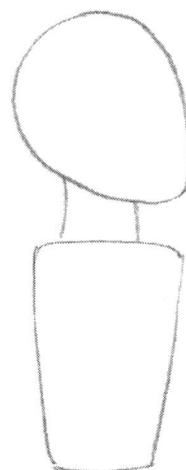

6 Draw the lower arms and legs.

7 Add hands and feet. Notice where each thumb is.

Even though the arms and legs are moving away from the body, the proportion of the figure is the same. Elbows meet the waist and hands come to mid-thigh.

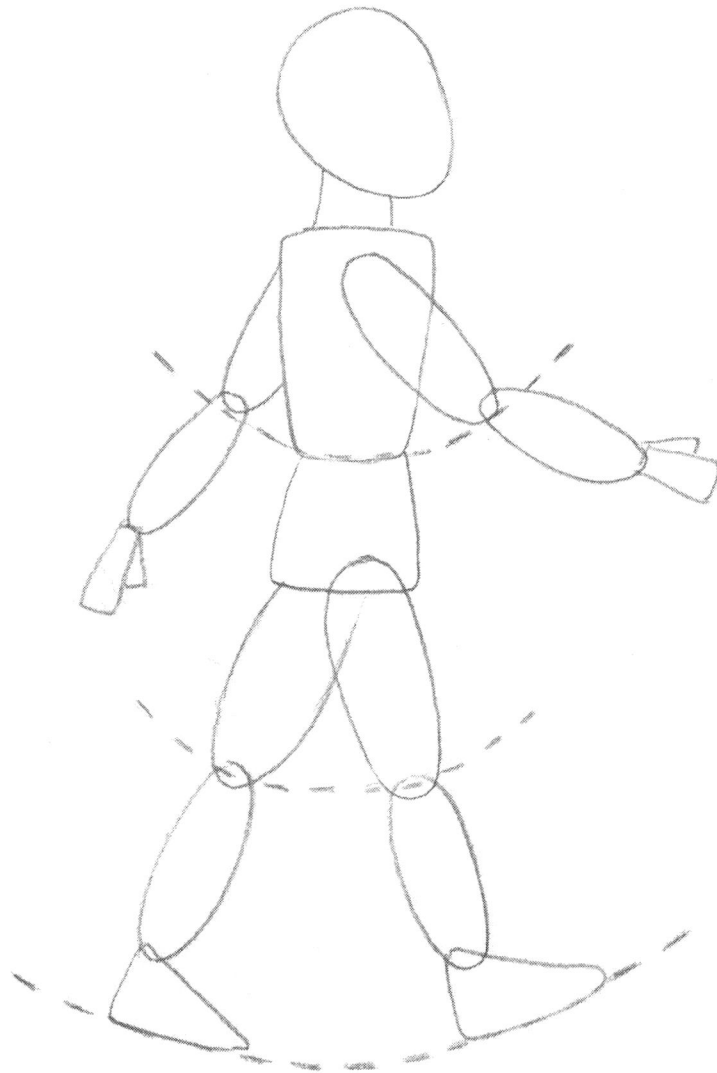

Proportion

To make a drawing of a person look
natural, it has to be in proportion.

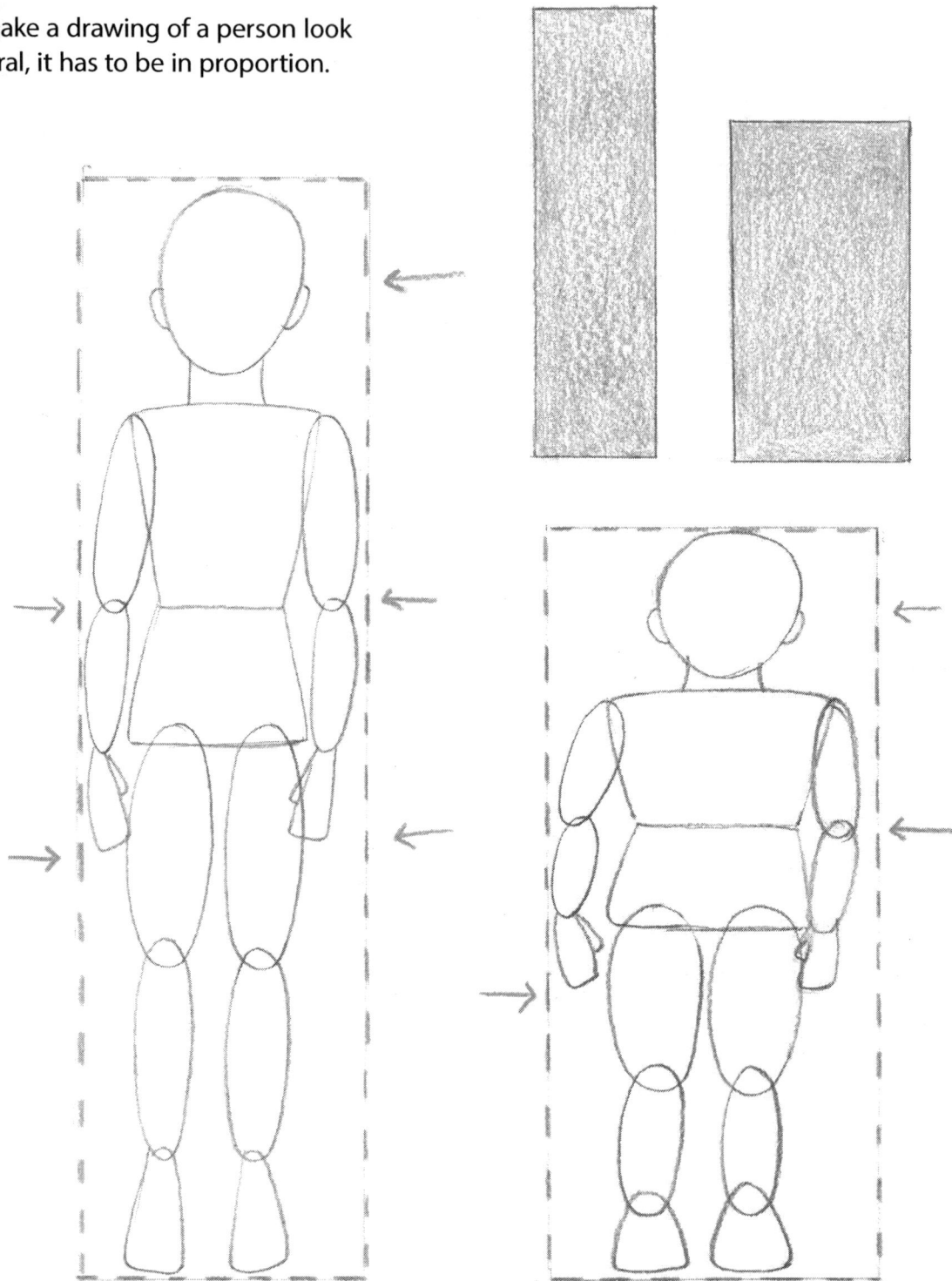

A person can be tall and thin or short and stout but elbows still meet
waist and hands still come to the middle of the thigh.

Faces
Front view

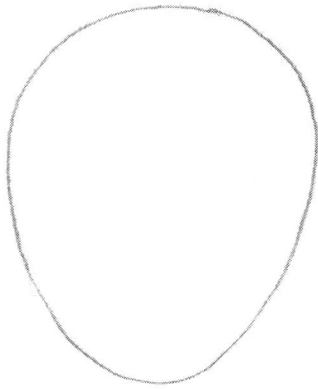

1 Start with an egg.

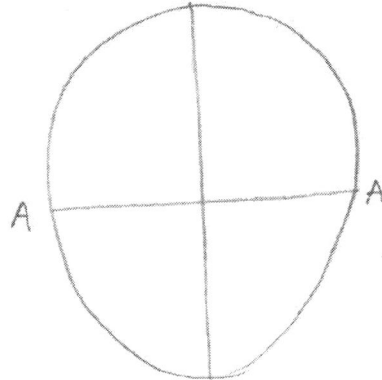

2 These guide lines should be drawn very lightly. Divide the egg horizontally and vertically.

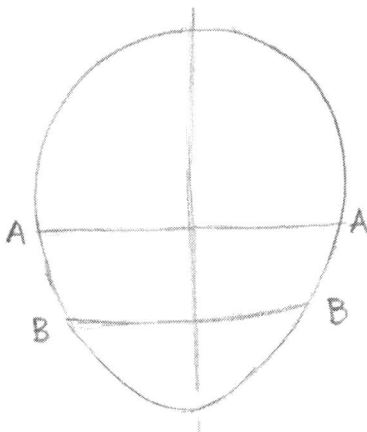

3 Divide the lower part of the face in half.

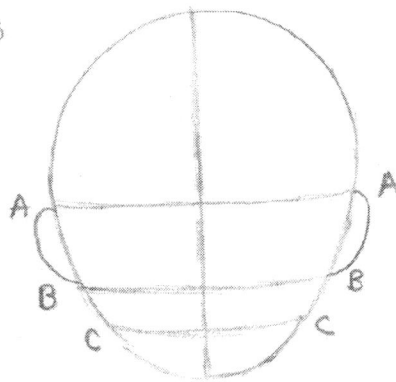

4 Divide the lowest part in half again. Ears are between line A and B.

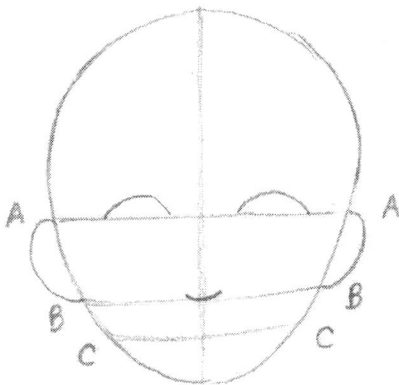

5 Eyebrows go above line A.

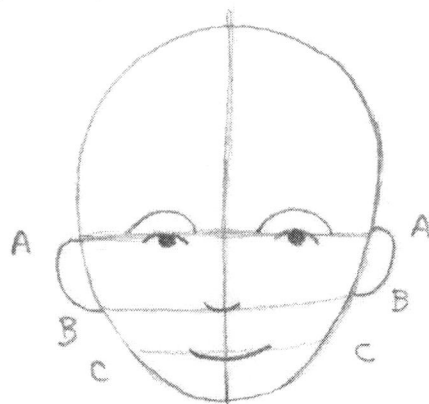

6 Eyes are on line A, The nose extends vertically from line A to line B. The mouth goes on line C.

Try different expressions. Notice what happens to the eyes and mouth. Eyebrows are very important to expressions. Use a mirror or ask a friend to model different expressions.

Try some of your own.

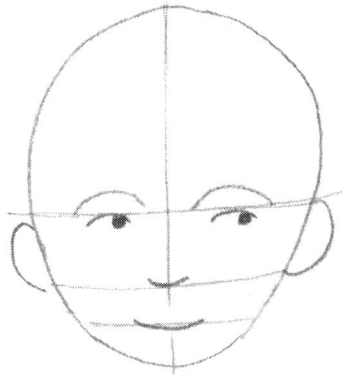

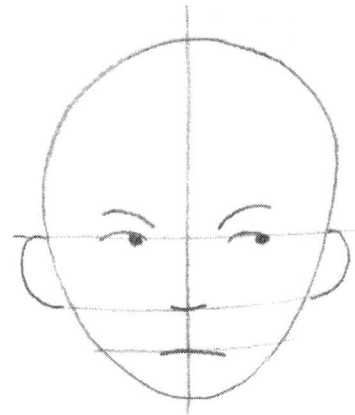

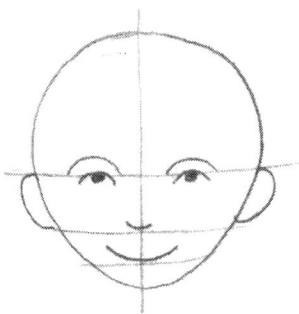

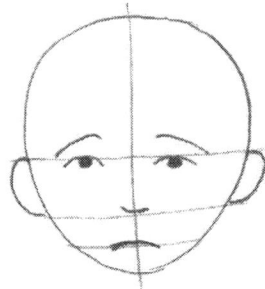

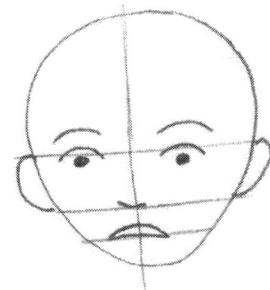

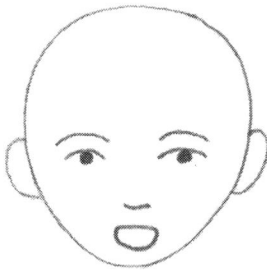

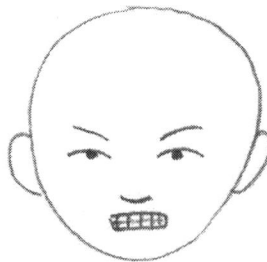

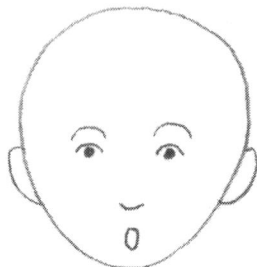

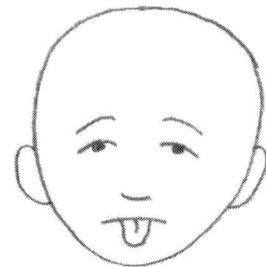

Faces
Side view (profile)

1   Draw an egg. Notice the angle of the egg.

2   Lightly draw line A.

3   Lightly add lines B and C.

4   The ear goes between line A and B in the middle of the head.

5   Add eyebrows above line A, and the nose is between line A and B.

6   Draw eyes just below line A and mouth is on line C.

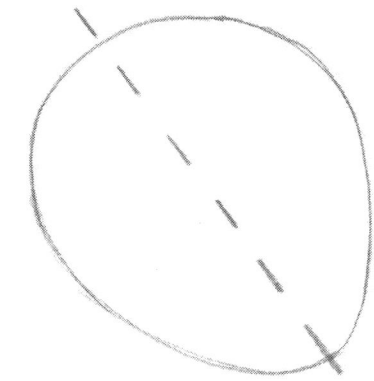

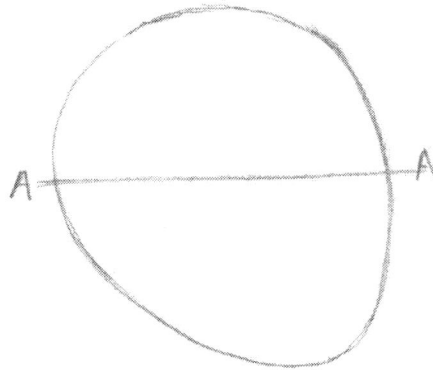

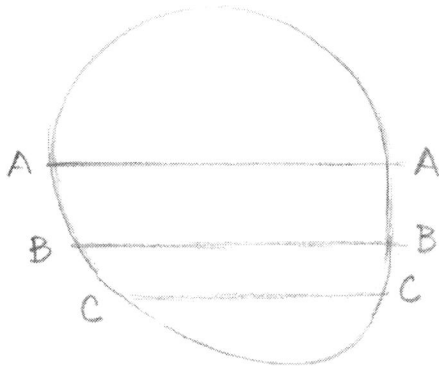

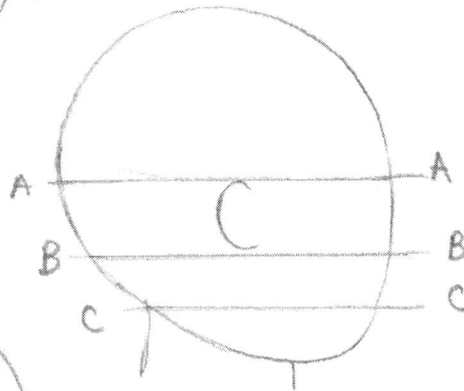

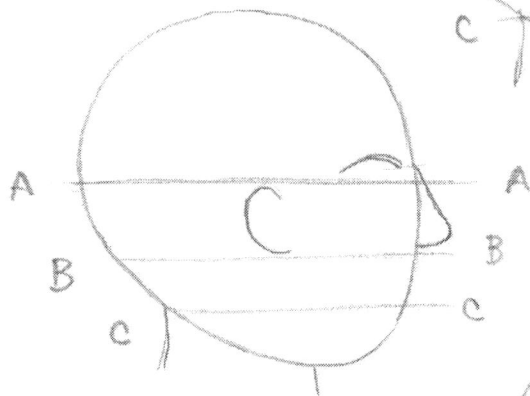

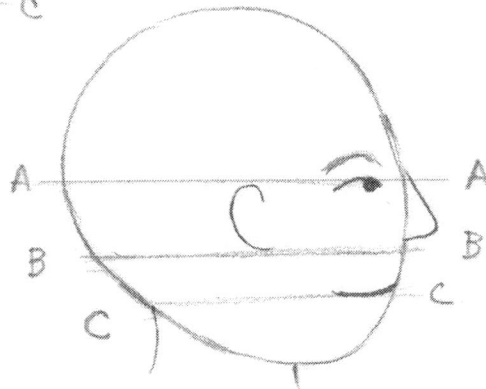

13

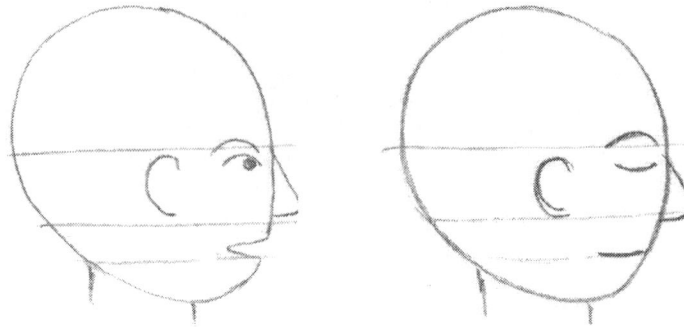

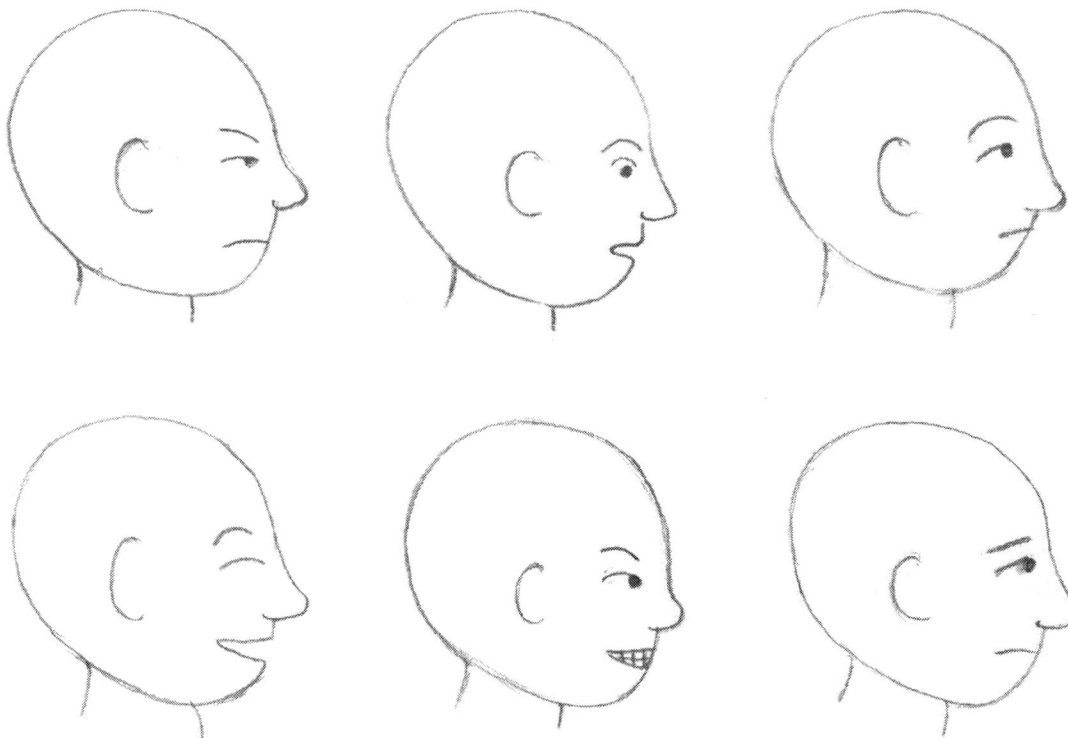

Try different expressions. With a friend, make
different facial expressions and draw each
other.

Remember: sketch lightly at first.

Hands

Here is a simple way to draw a hand.

1   Start with a trapezoid.

2   Add another trapezoid.

3   Divide the top trapezoid into four fingers.

4   Add a thumb.

1   Start with a trapezoid.

2   Add a thumb.

3   Add four fingers.

4   Erase extra lines.

15

Feet

1   Start with a trapezoid. This is a longer shape than the trapezoid you used for a hand.

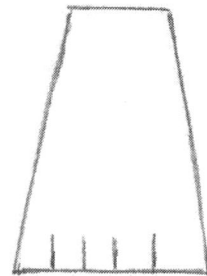

2   Draw short lines to show where the toes are. Remember: the 'big toe' is bigger than the rest!

3   Round off the shape of the toes.

4   Add toenails.

Side view of a foot:

1   Start with a triangle.

2   Add two lines for the ankle.

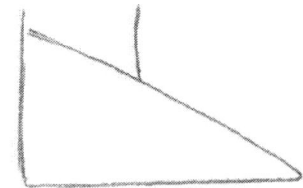

3   Round off the shape and erase extra lines.

4   Draw the curves on the bottom of the foot.

Skin color

People come in a great range of colors from light peach to dark brown and every shade in between.

Use your pencils to blend different skin colors. Remember, even if you decide to make all your people blue and green and purple, that's okay. Art is about observation and imagination. That means you can draw things that you see and you can also draw things that you make up.

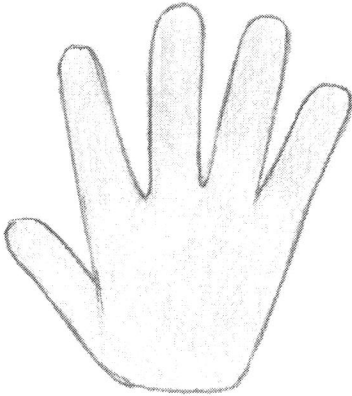

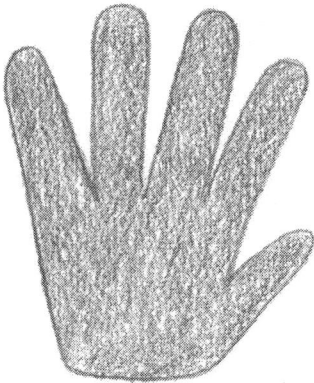

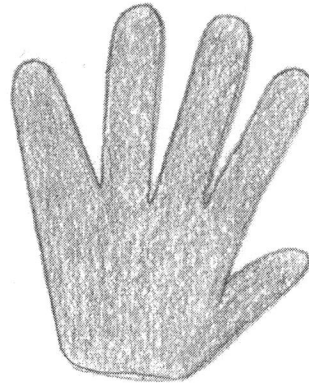

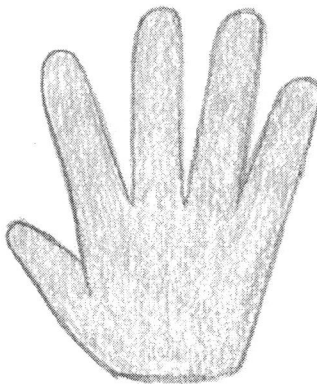

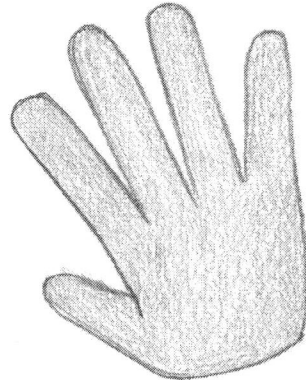

See color images at 123draw.com/color

Hair

People have straight hair, curly hair, or wavy hair. Hair can be blond or red or brown or black. People wear their hair long or short or loose or braided. Hair can be spike-y or smooth. People add beads and bows and barrettes. Some people dye their hair crazy colors like hot pink or green or blue. Look at the people around you and notice what their hair is like.

Now that you have practiced faces, draw a picture of yourself (SELF PORTRAIT). You can look in a mirror or at a photograph of yourself. What is your hair color? What is your eye color? What is your skin color? Is your nose big or small? Do you have freckles or rosy cheeks? Do you wear glasses? Do you have a favorite hat? Draw a portrait of yourself then draw portraits of your friends and family.

Now that you can draw a basic person, we will add ACTION. Each person starts with basic shapes. You can make it a boy or a girl and give it any kind of skin, hair, or clothes that you want.

18

See color images at 123draw.com/color

Person running

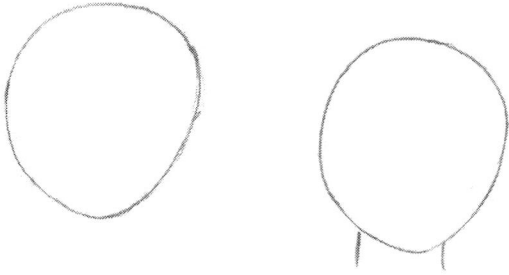

1 Start with an egg.

2 Add two lines for the neck.

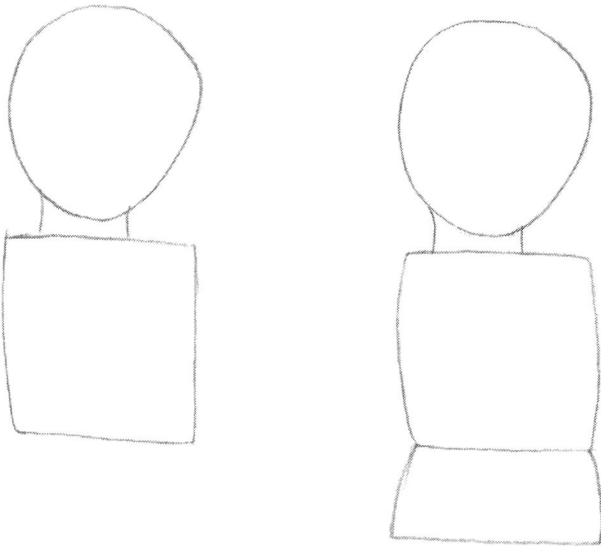

3 Draw the chest.

4 Draw the rest of the body.

5 Add the beginning of the two arms and two legs.

6 Draw the lower part of the arms and legs. Lightly draw guidelines on the head and add the eyes.

7 Finish the face. Add hands and feet.

8 Add the hair. Draw the clothes.

9 Erase all extra lines. Shade and color your running person.

Ballet dancer

Ballet is a form of dance that takes many years of serious training and hard work.

1   Start with an egg.

2   Add two lines for the neck.

3   Draw the chest.

4   Add ears and complete the body. Notice the angle of the second trapezoid.

5   Add the upper parts of the arms and legs.

6   Draw the face. Draw the lower parts of the arms and legs.

7   Draw hair. Add hands. Notice that her left hand is drawn to show her holding a wand. Draw feet. Female ballet dancers wear special toe shoes so they can dance on the tips of their toes.

8 Draw the ballet dancer's costume. Her skirt is called a 'tutu.'

9 Erase extra lines. Shade and color your ballet dancer.

See color images at 123draw.com/color

Soccer player

Soccer is a popular sport all over the world.

1   Start with an egg.

2   Add two lines for the neck. Draw the nose. This face will be in profile.

3   Draw a trapezoid for the chest.

4   Lightly draw guidelines for the face. Complete the face.

5   Complete the body with a second trapezoid. Draw the upper and lower arms. Draw the upper legs. Erase the extra lines of the face.

6 Finish the legs.

7 Add hands. Add feet.
Draw the hair.

8 Draw the soccer player's team uniform.

9 Erase extra lines. Shade and color your soccer player.

Long ago, my uncle played for the British team, Manchester United. Go Man-U!

Martial Arts

Most of the familiar forms of martial arts, such as Karate or Judo, originated in Asia. The color of the students belt tells how high a rank they have achieved.

1   Start with an egg. Notice the angle of the egg.

2   Draw the face.

3   Draw two lines for the neck. Draw the chest. Notice the angle of the chest.

4   Finish the body with a second trapezoid. Notice the angle of the trapezoid.

5   Draw the upper arms and upper legs.

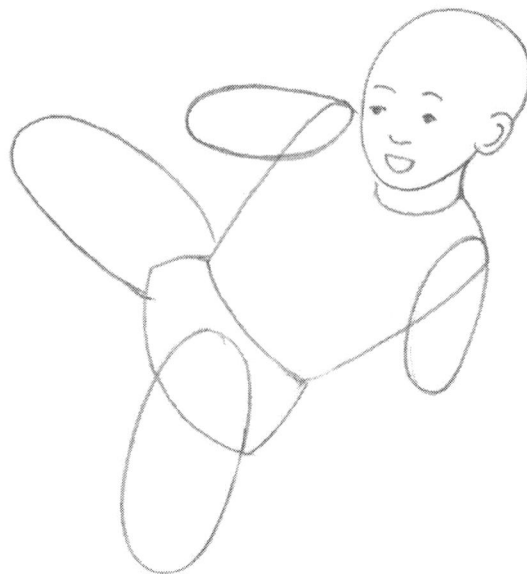

6 Draw the lower part of the arms and legs.

7 Draw the hands and feet. His feet are bare. This move is called a sidekick.

8 Draw the hair. Add the boys jacket and pants and belt. The jacket is called a "gi" (GEE as in GARDEN).

9 Erase extra lines. Shade and color your person. What color would you like the belt to be?

30

Gymnastics

The movements of gymnastics are designed to show strength, agility, and flexibility. This girl is learning a walkover on a practice beam which is only a few inches off the floor.

1   Start with an egg. Notice the angle of the egg.

2   Draw the face. Her head is in profile and looking down. Draw the neck.

3   Draw the chest.

4   Finish the body with a second trapezoid.

5   Draw the upper arms and legs.

6   Draw lower arms and legs.

7   Add hands. Notice where the
    thumbs are. Draw feet. Her feet
    are bare.

8 Draw hair. Gymnasts usually tie their hair back or wear it short so it does not get in their way. Erase extra lines and draw her team uniform.

9 Shade and color your gymnast. Draw her practice balance beam.

Great Gymnast!

Baseball player

Baseball is America's national sport. It is hard to imagine summer without it.

1 Let's draw the batter. Start with an egg.

2 Draw the face and ears. Notice that it is a 3/4 view of the face.

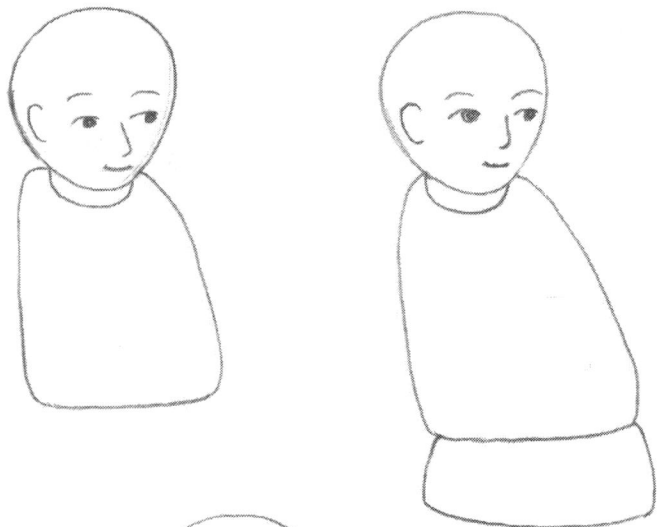

3 Draw the neck and chest.

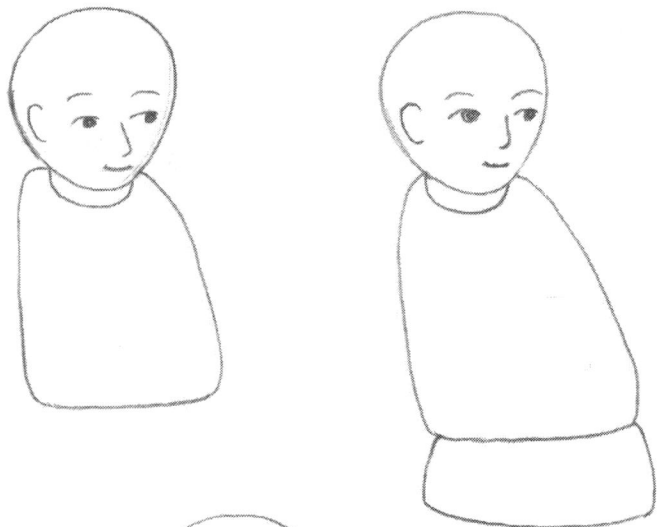

4 Finish the body with a second trapezoid.

5 Draw the upper arms and legs.

6 Draw lower arms and legs.

7 Look carefully at the position of the hands. Draw the hands. Draw the feet.

8 Draw a special protective hat called a batting helmet. Draw a tee shirt, pants and shoes. Draw the beginning of the bat.

9 Erase extra lines. Finish drawing the bat. Shade and color your baseball player.

Yoga

This boy is practicing yoga, an ancient system of exercises that help with strength, flexibility and balance. This pose is called 'Tree'.

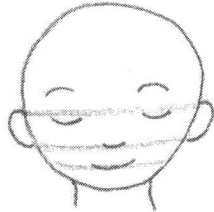

1   Draw an egg.

2   Draw the face and ears. Notice the eyes. They are drawn to show him looking down.

3   Draw the neck and chest.

4   Finish the body with a second trapezoid.

5   Draw the upper arms and legs.

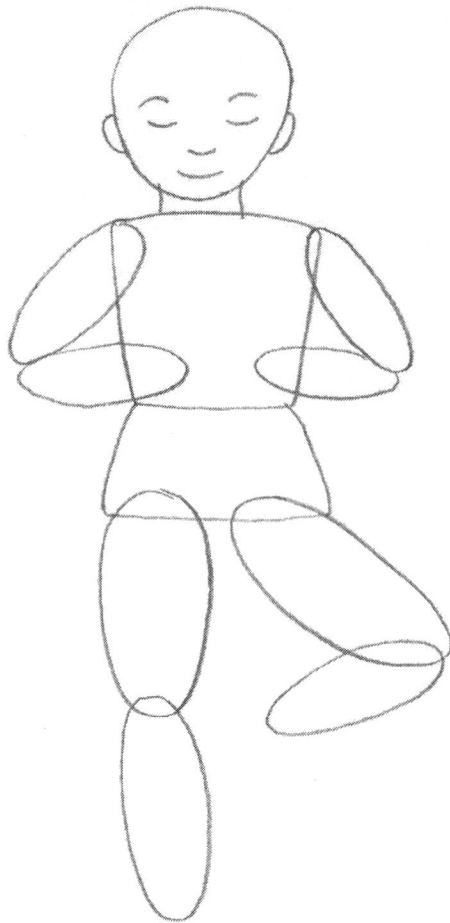

6 Draw the lower arms and legs.

7 Draw the hands and feet.

8 Draw hair. Draw his shirt and pants. Yoga is usually practiced barefoot on a special rubber mat.

10 Erase extra lines. Shade and color your boy practicing yoga.

Ice Skater

Figure skating is one of the most graceful sports to watch. Skaters practice long hours to make it look so smooth and easy.

1   Start with an egg.

2   Draw the face. Add two lines for the neck.

3   Draw the chest.

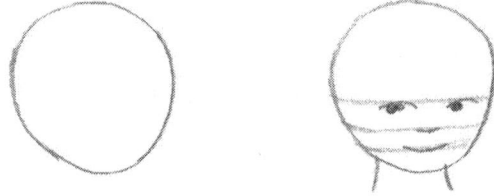

4   Finish the body with a second trapezoid. Notice the tilt of the second trapezoid.

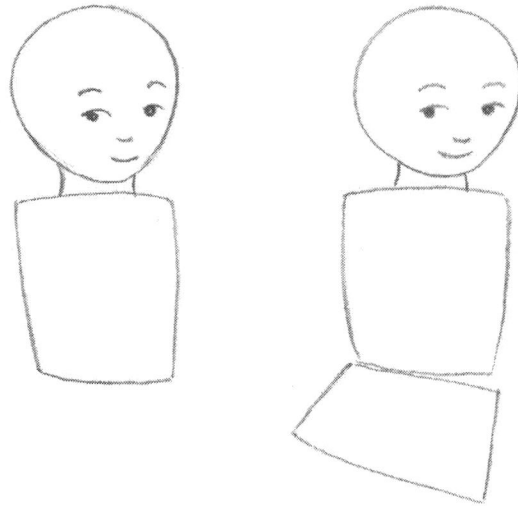

5   Add upper arms and legs.

6 Add hair. Draw the lower arms and legs.

7 Draw hands. Begin drawing the skates with a triangle.

8 Draw the ice skater's outfit. Draw the boots of the skates and the blades.

9 Erase extra lines. Shade and color your ice skater.

See color images at 123draw.com/color

Skateboarder

A skate board is just a board on wheels but skateboarders can do some amazing tricks on them. Wear your helmet!

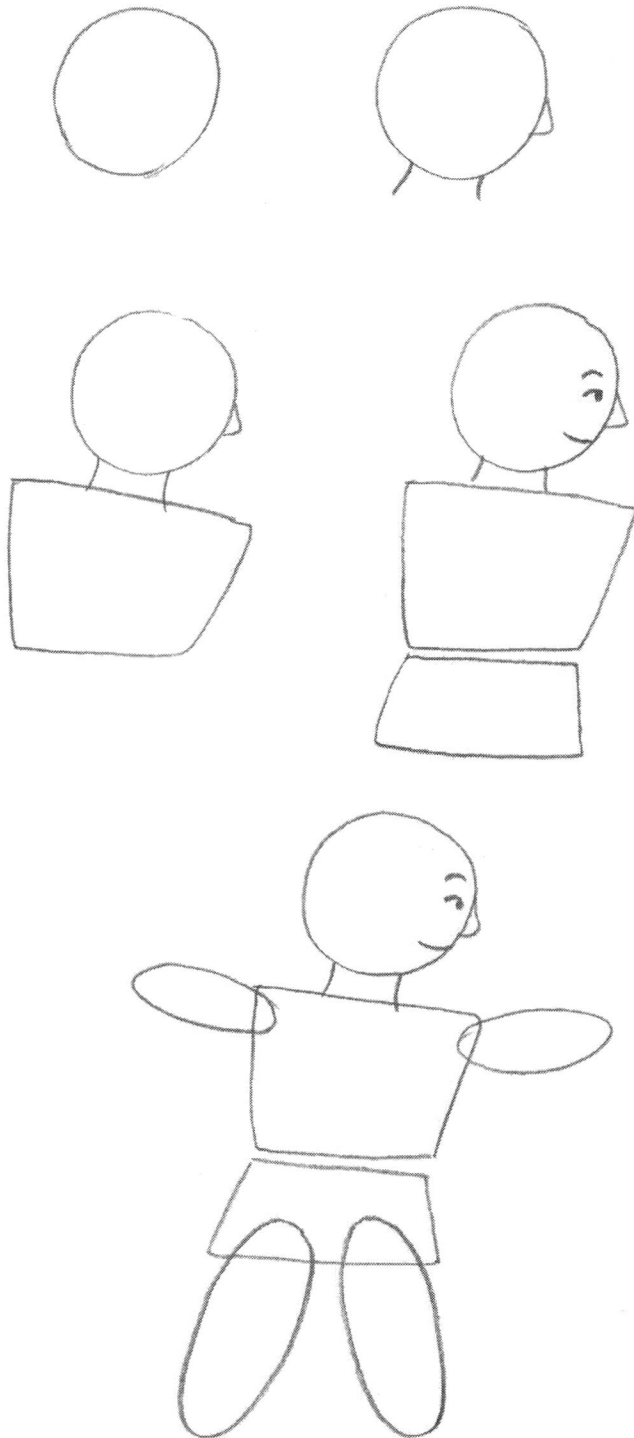

1   Start with an egg. This head will be in profile.

2   Draw a nose. Draw two lines for the neck.

3   Draw a trapezoid for the chest.

4   Finish the body with a second trapezoid. Draw the eyes and mouth.

5   Add upper arms and legs.

6 Draw lower arms and lower legs.

7 Draw the hands. Draw the feet.
  Add a skate board.

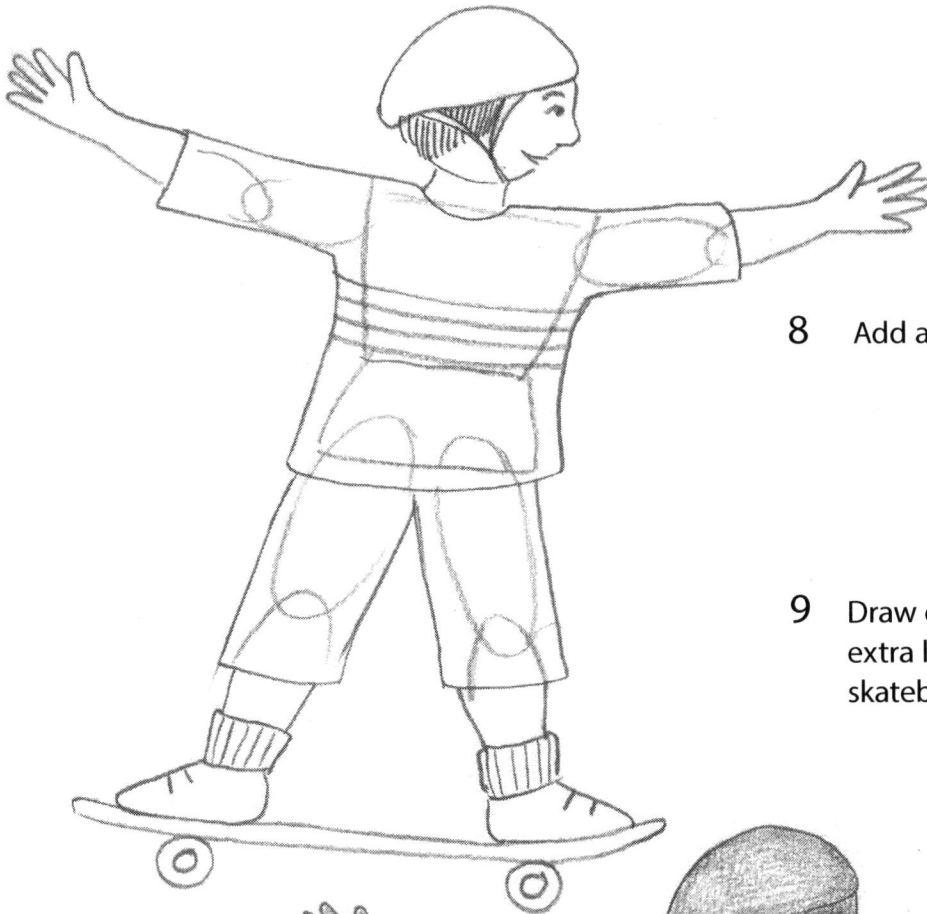

8 Add a helmet and hair.

9 Draw clothes and shoes. Erase extra lines. Shade and color your skateboarder.

Super skateboarder!

45

Bicycler

Bicycles are a great way to get around. People use bicycles all around the world.

Bicycles are also complicated to draw. Let's take it slow, step by step.

1   Start with an egg. This head will be in profile.

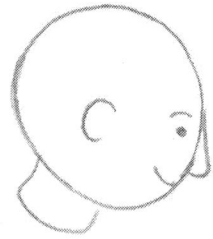

2   Draw the face and an ear. Add two lines for the neck.

3   Draw the chest.

4   Finish the body with another trapezoid. Notice how it is tilted.

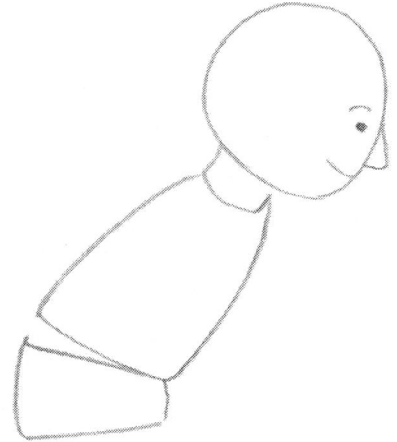

5   Draw the upper arms and legs.

6 Draw the lower legs and arms. Draw the hands and feet.

7 Erase extra lines. Draw a helmet and hair. Add a tee shirt and pants. Draw shoes.

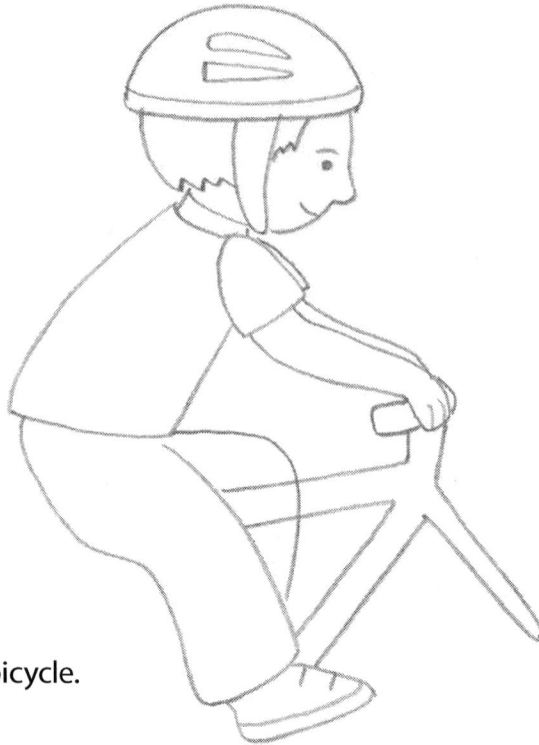

8 Begin the frame of the bicycle. Draw the front part and handlebars.

9 Draw the seat and rear frame.

10 Draw the wheels. Add a pedal under the boy's shoe.

11 Finish the details of the frame. Shade and color your bicycler.

Reader

Reading is one of my favorite things to do! This will give us a chance to draw a person sitting down.

1   Start with an egg. This face will be in 3/4 view.

2   Draw the face. Notice that the eyes are drawn looking down. Add an ear. Draw two lines for the neck.

3   Draw the chest.

4   Add a second trapezoid to finish the body. Notice the slight angle of the shape.

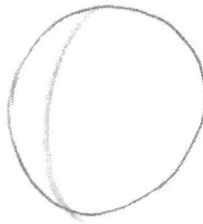

5   Draw upper arms and legs.

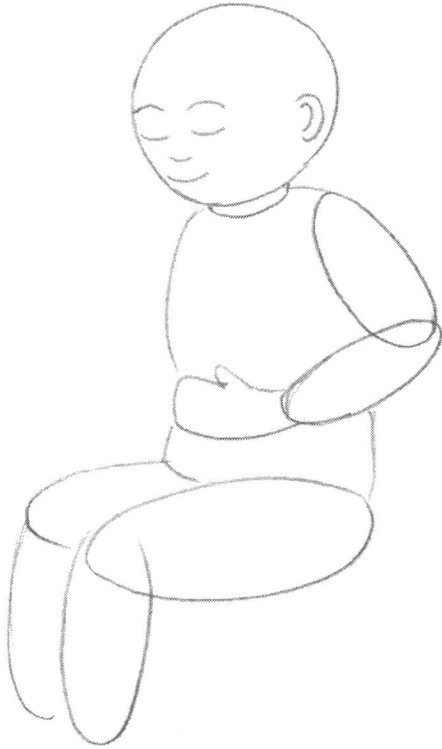

6   Draw the lower legs and arms.
Draw one hand.

7   Add hair. Draw the book the girl
is reading and her second hand.
Draw feet. Erase extra lines.

8   Add a stool for her to sit on.

9   Shade and color your reader.

I wonder what she's reading. What's your
favorite book?

Wheelchair basketball

This boy is disabled - he can't use his legs like other people. It doesn't stop him from playing basketball - he's a free-throw whiz!

1   Start with an egg.

2   Draw the face and an ear. Draw the neck.

3   Draw the chest.

4   Finish the body with a second trapezoid.

5   Draw the upper arms. Draw his legs.

6   Draw the lower arms. Draw the
    hands. Draw the feet.

7   Erase extra lines. Add hair. Draw
    a tee shirt. Draw the beginning
    of the wheelchair.

8   Finish the wheelchair by adding
    the wheels.

9   Finish his team uniform. Shade
    and color the basketball player.

Girl climbing

Sometimes it's fun to just play. This girl is playing on a climber at the park.

1   Start with an egg.

2   Draw the face and ears. Draw a neck.

3   Add the chest.

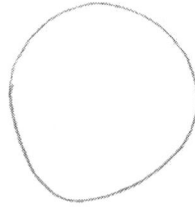

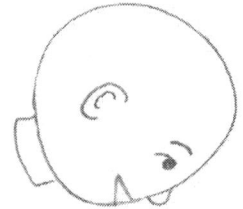

4   Add the lower torso. Erase lines to complete the face.

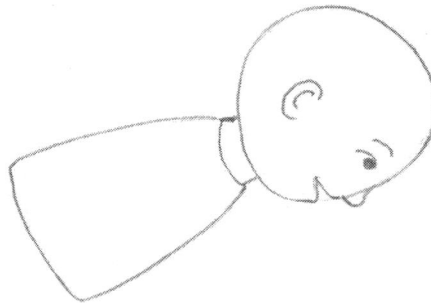

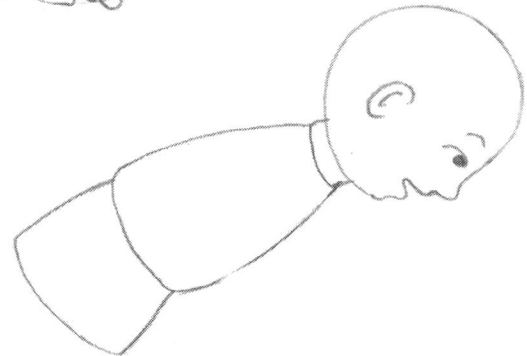

5   Draw the upper arms and upper legs.

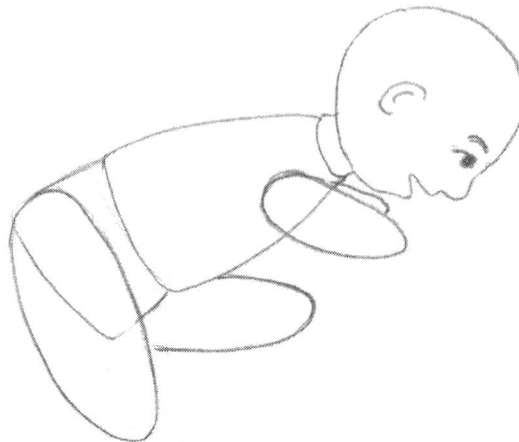

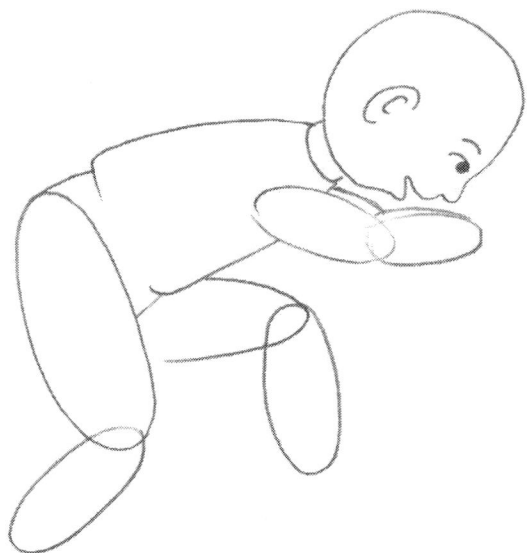

6   Draw the lower arms and legs.

7   Draw hands and feet.

8   Draw hair. Add clothes.

Girl jumping

1   Start with an egg.

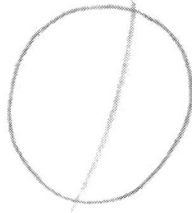

2   Draw the face. Draw an ear. Add
    the neck.

3   Draw the chest.

4   Finish the body with a second
    trapezoid.

5   Add the upper arms and legs.

58

6 Add the lower arms and legs.

7 Draw hands and feet.

8 Erase extra lines. Add hair and clothes.

Draw a climber. Color the jumping
and climbing girl.

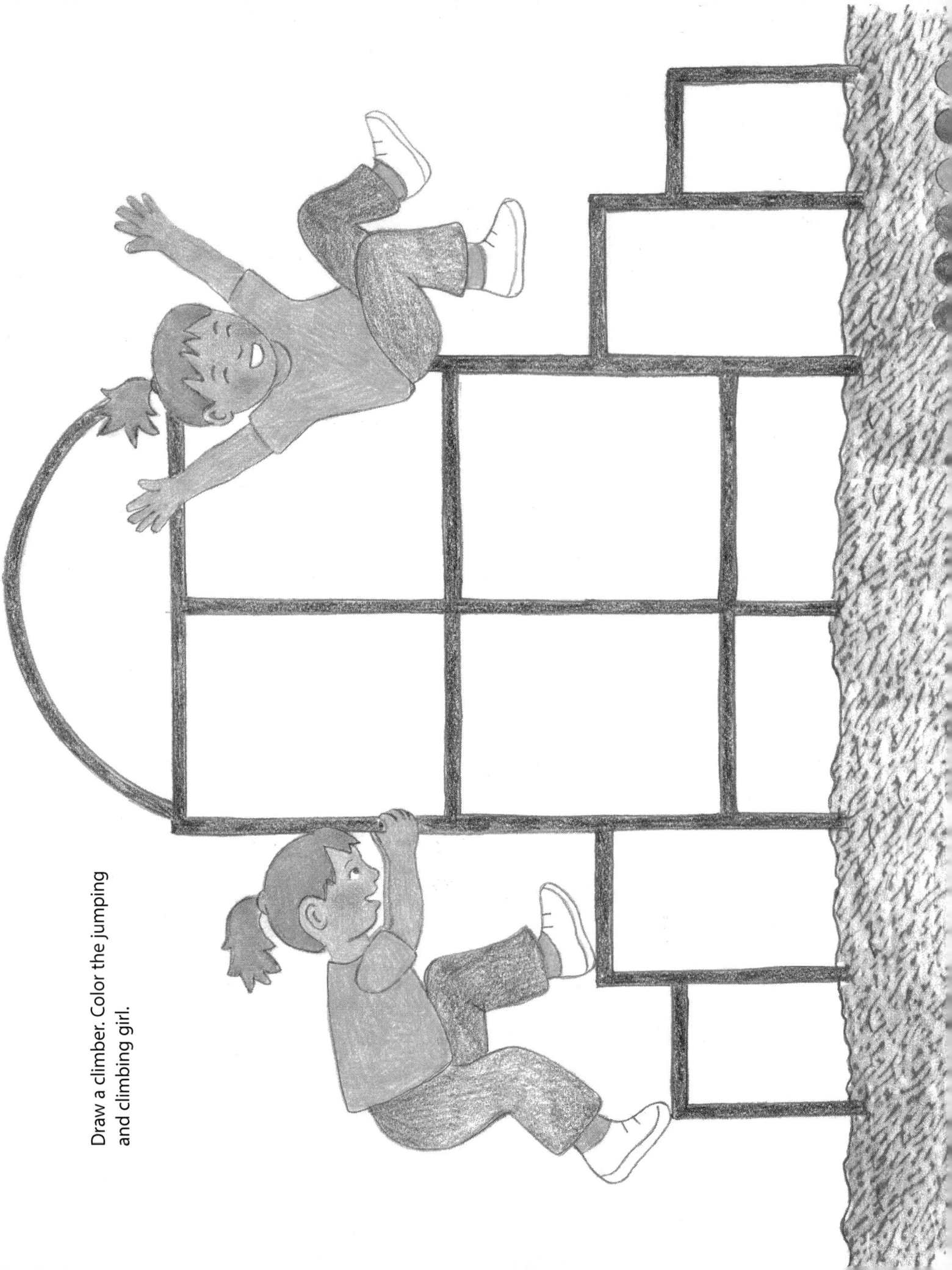

Artist

We can draw a picture of someone drawing a picture!

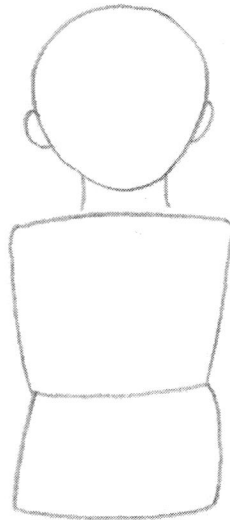

1 Start with an egg.

2 Add ears and a neck. This will be the back of her head.

3 Draw the chest.

4 Finish the body with a second trapezoid.

5 Add upper arms and legs.

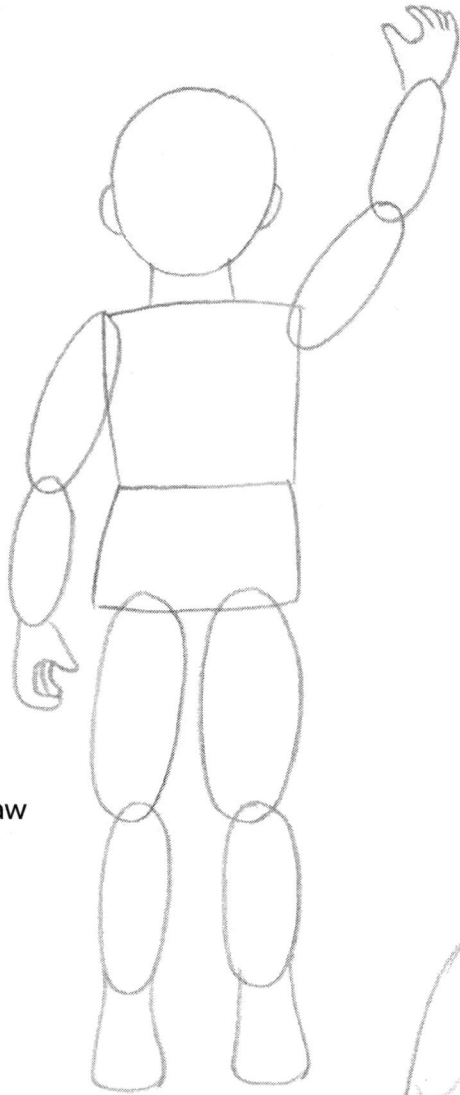

6 Add lower arms and legs. Draw hands and feet.

7 Draw hair. Add clothes.

Awesome artist, just like you!

8   Finish and color your artist.

9   Draw the front view.

Index

Made in the USA
Las Vegas, NV
05 November 2023